THE RECYCLING

Joey Connolly grew up in Sheffield, studied in Manchester and now works in London as the Director of Faber Academy. He received an Eric Gregory award in 2012, and his first collection, *Long Pass*, was published by Carcanet in 2017.

The Recycling

Joey Connolly

CARCANET POETRY

First published in Great Britain in 2023 by
Carcanet
Alliance House, 30 Cross Street
Manchester, M 2 7 A Q
www.carcanet.co.uk

A CIP catalogue record for this book is
available from the British Library.

ISBN 978 1 80017 319 4

Book design by Andrew Latimer, for Carcanet
Typesetting by LiteBook Prepress Services
Printed in Great Britain by SRP Ltd, Exeter, Devon

The publisher acknowledges financial
assistance from Arts Council England.

CONTENTS

SECTION I: TWO UNEDITED FIRST DRAFTS FROM THE TIME OF THE BREAK-UP

SECTION II: SOLVITUR AMBULANDO

SECTION III: PEOPLE, COUNTRYSIDES

SECTION IV: COUNTRYSIDES, PEOPLE

SECTION V: [...]

THE RECYCLING

THE RECYCLING

Strange noun full of verb, noun
bending to verb, strange
idea of repeating repetition,
repetition bending to noun,
to fixity, the plastic box full of
plastic boxes, strange self
full of other, the macrobiotic
yoghurt of nonself, pot
jogged and spilling into
itself, strange planet,
fractal mosaic of interintersecting
perspective, smoothie of
blueberries and theory, planet
bending to verb, being,
being doing, strange term,
the noncorporeal sexting
of looking at the trees, the
weekly imperative, imperative
bending to noun, as if right wasn't
the perpetual renegotiation of fog and
fog, noun
three quarters full, tending toward
not enough, what else?,
action bending towards
conviction, conviction's proxy,
cardboard of conviction, card
bending to more card, strange
toilet roll of pulped noughties slim-vols,
strange cycling of symbol and schema,
edge and node, just as matter
cycles already, cycled always, an always

always full of always, pushing
all its never to its outer edges
where it's most visible, strange
knowing which occludes or supplants its
knower, bending towards
a verb of oblivion
nounful of disembodied unsouled
feeling, jus of pillar-one being, it all is, strange
itself and not itself, vibrant
and shimmering with
anything, clinamen soup –

Thursday-night chore,
dust motes in a slope of light

'Word and form will be the board upon which I float atop billows of muteness.'
Clarice Lispector, *The Passion According to G. H.* (translated by Idra Novey)

'If at least I could just get them to grasp
that this quivering underneath us
means that we are walking on a bridge...'
Tomas Tranströmer, 'The Gallery' (translated by Robert Bly)

'And, looking at Albertine's mackintosh, in which she seemed to have become
another person, the tireless vagrant of rainy days, and which, close-fitting,
malleable and grey, seemed at that moment not so much intended to protect
her clothes from the rain as to have been soaked by it and to be clinging to her
body as though to take the imprint of her form for a sculptor...'
Marcel Proust, *Sodom and Gomorrah* (translated by Moncrieff and Kilmartin)

'For what admir'st thou, what transports thee so, / An outside?'
John Milton, *Paradise Lost*

'A poet in love must be encouraged in both capacities, or neither.'
Jane Austen, *Emma*

'All that is solid melts into air, all that is holy is profaned, and man is at last compelled to face with sober senses his real conditions of life, and his relations with his kind.'
Karl Marx and Friedrich Engels, *The Communist Manifesto*
(translated by Samuel Moore)

'Is a poet / An imperial dissident, or just / An outline / Of pale blue chalk?'
Bhanu Kapil, *How to Wash a Heart*

'[Tranströmer's poetry] enacts the qualities of a consciousness that knows it has been outside of time and is going to die, two thousand miles below words like *socialism* and *intentional anarchism* and *bankbook*, and it knows that the discovery and enactment of those qualities in our art are the spiritual precondition for a viable politics.'
Robert Hass, *Twentieth Century Pleasures*

'Maybe broken is just the same as being...'
Kei Miller, 'The Broken (II)'

'When I have bared myself, I feel a compulsion to send out a flurry of signals to adjust the reception of others, to scramble the image that may have been momentarily revealed of me –'
Nuar Alsadir, *Fourth Person Singular*

'The mind, that ocean where each kind
Does straight its own resemblance find;
Yet it creates, transcending these,
Far other worlds, and other seas;
Annihilating all that's made
To a green thought in a green shade.'
                    Andrew Marvell, 'The Garden'

'For all the nature of the primal atoms
Lies hidden far beneath our senses [...]
And fat lambs play and butt and frisk around.
We see all this confused and blurred by distance,
A white patch standing still amid the green.'
Lucretius, *On the Nature of the Universe* (translated by Ronald Melville)

'The artifacts and commodities that are conjured up by these desires
[cars, holidays etc] are, in a sense, at once expressions of and concealments of the
cultural matrix that brought them into being.'
                    Amitav Ghosh, *The Great Derangement*

'To turn back would have made sense
but I chose otherwise, a lamp post
at what I assumed was the golf course
a fixed point I couldn't seem to advance on,
like a failure of interpretation pursued because now

it is your life.'
                    Karen Solie, 'A Miscalculation'

'...the species we have chosen, historically, to protect are often those associated with damaged and impoverished places, and to defend them we must keep the ecosystem in this state.'
George Monbiot, *Feral*

'...thinking that emerges to cope with thoughts is not necessary when the ability to feel has not been frustrated.'
Nuar Alsadir, *Animal Joy*

'Just as, throughout the whole course of one's life, one's egoism sets before it all the time the objects that are of concern to the self, but never takes in that "I" itself which is perpetually observing them, so the desire which directs our actions descends towards them, but does not reach back into itself [...] the inertia of the mind urges it to slide down the easy slope of imagination, rather than climb the steep slope of introspection...'
Marcel Proust, *The Fugitive* (translated by Moncrieff and Kilmartin)

'...a metaphysics of that never objectifiable depth from which objects rise up towards our superficial knowledge...'
Michel Foucault, *The Order of Things* (translated by Alan Sheridan)

'...the wide-open pointless meaningless directionless dementia of the real.'
Anne Carson, 'Variations on the Right to Remain Silent'

'By the time I thought I really had to decide, I discovered the decision had already been made.'
Stuart Hall, *Familiar Stranger*

'I haven't even started yet and I'm already losing my nerve.'
Helen Oyeyemi, *Peaces*

'The bath cabin where you used to leave your dress
has changed forever into an abstract crystal [...]
Does it matter that we long for things as they are in themselves?'
Czesław Miłosz, 'Elegy for N. N.' (translated by Czesław Miłosz and Lawrence Davis)

'Ah, what a dusty answer gets the soul
When hot for certainties in this our life! –
In tragic hints here see what evermore
Moves dark as yonder midnight ocean's force,
Thundering like ramping hosts of warrior horse,
To throw that faint thin line upon the shore!'
George Meredith, *Modern Love*

'...any contentment on one point or another of our enquiries consists only in a
sort of dreaming resignation as we paint the walls within which we sit out our
imprisonment with bright figures and vistas of light...'
Johann Wolfgang von Goethe, *The Sorrows of Young Werther*
(translated by David Constantine)

'The world is a looking-glass, and gives back to every man the reflection of his
own face.'
William Makepeace Thackeray, *Vanity Fair*

'Our brains create our worlds through processes of Bayesian best guessing in
which sensory signals serve primarily to rein in our continually evolving percep-
tual hypotheses. We live within a controlled hallucination which evolution has
designed not for accuracy but for utility.'
Anil Seth, *Being You*

'The imagination, filler of the void, is essentially a liar. It does away with the third dimension, for only real objects have three dimensions. It does away with multiple relationships.'
Simone Weil, *Gravity and Grace* (translated by Arthur Wills)

'... "enargeia," which means something like "bright unbearable reality." It's the word used when gods come to earth not in disguise but as themselves.'
Alice Oswald, Introduction to *Memorial*

'We live nearly always through screens – a screened existence.
And I sometimes think when people say my work is violent that from time to time I have been able to clear away one or two of the screens.'
Francis Bacon, in an interview with D. Sylvester

'Perhaps what is inexpressible (what I find mysterious and am not able to express) is the background against which whatever I could express has its meaning.'
Ludwig Wittgenstein, *Culture and Value* (translated by Peter Winch).

'But if the human being is to find his way once again into the nearness of being he must first learn to exist in the nameless.'
Martin Heidegger, 'Letter on Humanism'
(translated by Frank A. Capuzzi and J. Glenn Gray)

'Hospitality is the highest expression of a universal reason that has come into its own. Reason does not exercise any homogenizing power. Its *friendliness* enables it to acknowledge the Other in their otherness and welcome them.'
Byung-Chul Han, *The Expulsion of the Other* (translated by Wieland Hoban)

'It's sad, something coming to an end. It cracks you open, in a way – cracks you open to feeling. When you try to avoid the pain, it creates greater pain. I'm a human being, having a human experience in front of the world.'
Jennifer Aniston, to *Vanity Fair*, September 2005

'The fiction is already there. The writer's task is to invent the reality.'
J. G. Ballard, Introduction to *Crash*

'Send forth / The flame of thy desire, so that it issue /
Imprinted well with the internal stamp.'
Dante Alighieri, *Paradiso* (translated by Henry Wadsworth Longfellow)

'When another kind of fire with a faster motion falls on the visual ray and penetrates it right up to the eyes, it forces apart and dissolves the passages in the eyes, and causes the discharge of a mass of fire and water which we call a "tear"…'
Plato, *Timaeus and Critias* (translated by Desmond Lee)

'I am tired of satisfying my desire for murder stealthily by admiring the imperial pomp of sunsets.'
Jean Genet, *Our Lady of the Flowers* (translated by Bernard Frechtman)

'…a harp, its string cutting / deep into my palm. In the dream, /
it both makes the wound and seals the wound.'
Louise Glück, 'Fugue'

'He lay, panting heavily in the wet air, and tried feeling bits of himself to see where he might be hurt. Wherever he touched himself, he encountered a pain. After a short while he worked out that this was because it was his hand that was hurting.'
Douglas Adams, *Life, the Universe and Everything*

'We all know which suffering is meant to be ours.'
Sheila Heti, *Motherhood*

'The death toll is always one, plus one, plus one, plus one. The death toll is always one.'
Teju Cole, *Blind Spot*

'...one must begin sometime...'
Zelda Fitzgerald, *Save Me the Waltz*

'Formalism was part of the strategy – like asbestos gloves, it allowed me to handle material I couldn't pick up barehanded.'
Adrienne Rich, *Arts of the Possible*

'The craftsman and his artefact thwart each other.'
Michel de Montaigne, 'On Repentance'
(translated by M. A. Screech)

'...how, gradually, what could not be taken away
is taken. People, countrysides.'
Czesław Miłosz, 'Elegy for N. N.' (translated by Czesław Miłosz and Lawrence Davis)

DATA

Turing memorial   bitten apple   January appleblossom

SECTION I: TWO UNEDITED FIRST DRAFTS FROM
THE TIME OF THE BREAK-UP

SOLVITUR AMBULANDO
'It is solved by walking'

Run to the country to lick the wound we've made of our relationship
can it be a sign that I'm confronted off the train
by an endless cemetery? Or is it more a sign
that I'm perceiving the world in terms of signs,
outsourcing the burden of sense-making onto the canvas of stuff
and emptying myself of agency and therefore of culpability

or is it more a sign that I find this explanation?
Christ, the industrial solvent of reason,
every muddy ramble a posy of pointing fingers,
scattering their direction like a pissed-up Herzog.
In the cemetery the trees are alight with their own
decline, cheering feebly in apricot and plum and sage.
If I'm ending this I have to protect what we had,
I would not survive its erasure. Do you seriously believe,
fourteen lines in, that there's still a decision to be made?
The gorge of clarity rises in my throat. The cavalry is in disarray,

the infantry breaking formation, the pennants in
beautiful tatters. He's going to walk. He's going to walk, he's going
off, look, like a dog narrating the flung stick,
Jesus. The trees are nothing like the frozen burst of fireworks, no matter
how often I try to say so. The trees
are lit like meteors by their own descent.
Can I really do this? Really brick the phone of my heart?

UN PICCOLO DIVERTIMENTO

The challenge is knowing how to know. The challenge
is mechanistic and archetypal in its chattering columns
of pros and cons, of precedent and a kind of carnal *bodmas*.
The challenge is in how to stop your mouth convulsing into
its grotesque organic trapezoid as you lose it in the shower,
your mouth filling up with water. The challenge is
to balance between the weighing scales and the spectacles
and the outboard motor. The challenge is therefore
epistemological, a razorblade run along a seam you didn't know
you had. The challenge is to run *Doom* off a potato's chemical energy,
the challenge is pitch and stake, the raw treacle
which plugs up the gaps between the rubber-band-and-paperclip
miscellany of dailiness, the humdrum rattlebag of
grubby window-frames and contentment, the asymmetric
mushroom up of oatmilk in the teacup, the abrasive
chord of other people's children as you sit, semi-consciously
picking at the loose seams of your inherited greatcoat. The challenge,
this Spanish villa having the wrong type of vegetable peeler,
is where to start the fire. Apollo, Bacchus, find some other playground –
I didn't sign up to walk this tightrope. The challenge is reconciling the
triple threat of the righteous dissatisfaction which facilitates ambition
or just the dregs of motivation which drag you from bed –
with the ragged umbrella – with the blinding light.
The challenge was to run from doom
on the vegetable oil–powered jalopy of love. The challenge
has to do with why you're writing your suicide note
in Esperanto: why must you fuck off the analysts?
Why are you pushing yourself backward through the rose garden?,
planking secretly amid pyramidal stacks of
I-beams in weekend-abandoned city-centre construction sites.

Why did you bioengineer the new apple
and leave it to moulder in the icebox? What made you tell the class
to spend a term drawing pictures of purgatory? What made you crack
   that massive
joke? Why burn the origami cacti? How has all this
water got in? Why did you both pedal your tricycles out to the
godforsaken service station? Why? Why? Why? How? Why? Why?

SECTION II: SOLVITUR AMBULANDO

OKM (BREAK-UP CENTO)

I haven't been feeling emotional lately, really I haven't.
Am I lonely? Yes. Am I upset? Yes. Am I confused?

Being able to go to the water's edge and scream –
I kind of love that not knowing. It's seamless;

somewhere along the way, you sort of lose yourself.
The world was shocked, and I was shocked.

I have my imaginary dog cone on, so I don't see anything.
It's important for me not to read anything, not to see anything,

It's sad, something coming to an end.

Brad and I used to joke that every piece of furniture
was a museum piece. There are many stages of grief.

You have marriages within marriages within marriages.
That's quite a backyard, in my opinion.

1KM (DISSOLUTION)

I will admit there is more than one passage
by which light may be transmitted unto the world.
If primarily our father, hallowed in his heaven.
But He has allowed that all things curve

and all bend, and in this manner
that light be brought up and held
against the dark, like a human palm
to the timeless gritstone of our monastery wall.

It's said the new king mulls our dissolution. You,
for example, a Leonardo's sketchbook of curves,
a lifetime's study of gradient and swell, the flash of a shadow
as you depart, at dawn. This time, forever. Another curve.

For months I pace the kitchen garden, pondering the leeks;
that apostate at Nonsuch; the heresy *deus otiosus*
and Brother Tarewell's howling in his sleep. And, helpless,
I requiem your skin, your shoulder blades. Your – back.

As the abbot's nacre pyx is japped with goldlight,
I know a blaze of malediction glisters my impious mind
when I reckon thus: primarily our Lord, but also
you, old friend. You also are a source of light. Farewell.

2KM (THE YEAR OF THE SCYTHE)

No, Pierre, the Contessa has left us.
Fled. Chef too: that curdled reek is the milkpan
boiled dry on the range. Or else it is our visitors:
their 'third estate' is at the walls. I confess
I cannot face the thought without despair.

Either thought, Pierre. A noble, timeless peasantry
riled – to what end?! – by cynics and decadents,
that *Parisienne* academy of clowns, automata and vipers.
They perorate their bile of meaningless ideals
to feed a hunger in the rabble that they never knew they felt.

Never knew. Can you imagine a gladder state
than sunken in the fine wine of the old ways,
stupor of root spread from root, for a fiveyear or time immemorial,
the numb swoon of continuity below the skin of things,
the uninflected wheeling rhythm of the seasons,

decades swelling and ceding like
cows circling in the pasture, silent, dumb-
love-eyed. Lives and generations arriving and passing off
like shoals of fish coalescing and dissolving
in the fathomless dark of the Atlantic;

the drowse of likeness, tomorrow cosseted to today
like a crosspiece coupling in its yoke,
and the iron tide of winter rising again or falling,
stern black-coated tutor to its nursling nature.
Oh, Pierre!, the damp clean spell of wild garlic

passaged on the cold night air,
a sky of aubergine and burgundy above them
as they tramp homeward from the fields, the air,
the vast sky and the fields running parallel
forever. It is a heaven, is it not? To be

correct, Pierre, for your station, to feel
the ebb of eons at the corner of the mind.
Let them refuse the iron plough!, and continue
with the wood; they think we trick them,
and perhaps we do. We disabuse them

not of money but of all connection to the land. Perhaps
we are, Pierre, no better than the Jacobins – but slower, slower.
What coin is spent in revolution? The laughing picnics
of the farmgirls, good comté in greased paper
and brown string, the plaintive music of the mountain goats

creaking from the hillsides of the Haute-Savoie.
Or the autumn rain, battering at a simple cape
or the low slate or thatch of weathered hovels.
The hissing of the sheaves of grain, Pierre,
settling one against another in the moonlight,

the silken passage of the scythe in the offices
of its proper ministry. Oh Pierre, a decorous eternity
is sacrificed on the gaudy altar of tomorrow!
They claim to suppose we hate and fear the new:
not so. It is merely that, unlike they,

we do not lack the appetitive sensibility
for the voluptuous appeal of ages, the savour of epoch.
The Greeks knew it; their beloved Romans knew it well.
Take the Contessa, Pierre – what dispirits me
is not so much the absence of her body,

as the departure with her body of the living history
between us, which even now is failing. Overwritten, Pierre,
by that deathly revisionist historian
named Time. The peasants required no new page.
The homely muck and squalor, into which,

tick-like, they're burrowed; the kettle whistling at sun-up
the glad sentinel of continuity. Even this,
Pierre, has its greatness. Like a leaden word in a poem
smithied into gold by its line, so they are ennobled
by the manner of relation to a seigneur

and their ordination thereby into our *ancien regime.*
That brightly lit tunnel through the alp of history,
surrounded on all sides by the fearful press of mute rock-matter,
the inhuman muteness and nullity outside culture,
the infinite stifling darkness — oh,

forgive me, Pierre, I am become carried away. I couldn't
trouble you for the evening editions, could I?
No, no, I couldn't – and anyway they are no longer
printed. But I fancied how the Contessa and I – for all our
bicker and dither over the riddles in the dailies –

that we might uphold our stanchion
in the long colonnade of history, the noble book of man and,
precisely through that ballast and fuse-point
of these hayseeds so gallingly battering the gates, of nature too.
This revolution consumes its materials like a conflagration,

and one material is the mechanism of interface between
man and beast, man and sky, man and soil. Man, Pierre,
and son. Their wretched calendar unpeels past from present,
is a fracture at the very secret heart of truth.
(The mechanism, Pierre, is known as *sublimation*:

they despise this or that in their own lives
and so tear down the world entire and start anew.)
The truth! The truth is she was leaving anyway,
Pierre. Chef too. I am concerned that it is under
my fleeting stewardship, Pierre, that our family name,

traceable to the early days of Montmorency, Pierre,
shall be let slip —— or I'm not, Pierre. I grow tired.
I can hardly sustain the rhythm of pretence. Ah!,
I hear the gates are burst, at last. No matter, Pierre,
the guillotine has snickered in Paris since May. Would you be so good,

Pierre, to find my coat, my stick. We have a walk to make,
Pierre. A walk to make, and a telegraph to deconstruct.

3KM (LITTLE GEORGE WAS AFTER ALL)

Little George is after all was only eight
but an expensive education had equipped him with the
vocabulary if not quite the proper sensibility –
though where in the end is the distinction –
to remark with apparent perspicacity
upon the rapidly changing architecture of Vienna's fashionable suburbs.
And if there was something… unsettling
in the hungry precocity of his commentary
on the thoroughfares of the noble quarter – well, who would plug that
gushing fount, what kind of person?
The boy was eight. I do not regret
indulging him. Reticence a little toolkit of its own. Little George,
in a photo of him, one of few, helpless in short trousers and his
military-style dress jacket: you get the sense in retrospect he felt himself
trussed, just vaguely: a lupine gleam at the cornea,
a cold Nietzschean touch of his mother
in the way he stretches his lips as he waits
for someone out of frame to finish speaking. His mother became
indisposed, of course, when he was very young – the good doctor
hadn't yet taught us to weigh these things
properly, in that benighted decade, and Lithium quite the thing.
He did really have something to say
about the new parades being constructed
in the Leopoldstadt or Margareten – I owned a house there, myself,
before I cut things off with the creature
in the sanatorium, lost my position
at her father's firm. But Georgie had things left to say. I believe it was the fact
that even the heaviest structures of stone and iron
might be torn down, like paper, and replaced
that so obsessed his little heart. But George – he was
the only remaining product of our summer years, is how I felt.

And so I took a perhaps unusual – some would same unhealthy – tutelage
of the boy – his schooling in the latest science;
in chemistry, phrenology, toxicology, aviation –
that he may have everything he need for this cold world.
A little overmuch, I concede, for a boy of seven.
But anyway – all of that will go to waste now, I suppose.

4KM (FURNESS VALE)

The lord up the manor and his bowler-hats
had a new chemical for the coal
and for week our Bill was brighter
with the hope we might stay open yet,
the oaken knots of his hands unloosing
more quickly after a day at the face.
He took butter again in his tea;
whistled his gravelled whistle. Maybe

we had another decade in us, this ugly village
which feels as old as its hills
and isn't. For a while again
he'd splash with the little ones
in the new aluminium tub, pattercake.
In one day he reblacked the scuttle,
we fucked, he called round Ella's, took them
Herb's old cradle. Pointed out to me the sky's
blue and silver sprawl, his warm breath
billowing in the air between the banks of the lane.

Then a blast took two women's husbands
and it all came down again. Like he could find
nothing to breathe but blackdamp.
And what am I to do? The man I married,
he had a pounce to him. What am I to do?
I can do a tea from the ends of yesterdays,
but cannot bring heat from cold coals. I cannot.
Down the alley to the blackened chapel
the competing scents of saxifrage and ash-pit mix
into something bitter and untellable.
Oh, the fearful ca'canny of the heart...

We lived embedded deep within the mid-late mesolithic,
our little tight-knit band of kin and quasi-kin,
though we'd have hardly called it that. We had
one word. It meant: to live within something
beautiful and whole, but perilous, hard.
One quiet child lost a finger knapping flint –
by autumn he was dead. I remember most the fascination
with the bones of smaller creatures – anything big enough
you'd carve into people fucking – but the small bones:
we loved those for themselves. Looking back
I think what drew us
was the sense that underneath the skin of things
there was a structure, which was complex but coherent,
delicate, and interlinked. Not that we had
the words for this. And the bones could be used for making
new patterns, too. Even the Neanderthals knew this
and had their own rough practice of abstractionism –
the baseline I see now which every visionary endeavour
both rises out of and returns – only
their artworks didn't have a place to land. Expression without
return or reciprocation: is that survivable? We require
something back, or we'll be worn down until there's nothing left.
They subsided into listless anomie and were subsumed.
The stance required for survival long-term was of not being
outside of, but neither swallowed by
the world within which we existed. To be the trembling skin.

We could flay and tan, of course, but you .
never got it all, the edgings of muscle and the reek of life,
before it got cold out and we needed them for warmth.
We'd wrap ourselves in what it was we'd killed.
The cave paintings were the same.

Though we'd have hardly put it that way. At any time
you can't see what it is you've got. Poor soul.
And afterwards its truth is utterly concealed, hidden as a skeleton
in something living. Or previously living. Like you and me.

Abstracted, ankle deep in the proto-gutters of Elizabethan London:
how were you ejected from your life to wash up here?
The question flattens in the flicker of passing nights.
Mice crackle and nest in the thatch, poets brawl in the hostelry.

Perfume and French from off the passing courtiers on horseback
barely mask the rank airs of shit and English.
Alehouse theologies clog the street corners with sulfur
and verdant departed gardens. Moments of consciousness raise
from the flatlands of dailiness like low Golgothas
but, increasingly, you belong.

The architecture pitches alarmingly over the horsedrawn gridlock
carrying its load of turnip, skirret and cabbage, rusting
miscellanies of ironwork waif-pilfered off the docks. Then less alarmingly.

You spurn the tavern for the markets, cast and anneal
a new soul to be cushioned by the symbiotic rhetorics
of godliness and cleanliness. Though it be a struggle.
You have a favourite recipe: it's stew. You cure. You coppice.
You structure minute routines for your every day. It helps.

Flax and hemp ripen the summer air with their seamy exhalations
from the city gardens. Realism is the thing; not romance. Breathe it in
and keep your head down. Sharpen the knife you keep in your boot.
Befriend the waifs. This Shaxpard will have to show himself eventually.

7 K M

Imperial Japan–era wood and paper pagodas glide by
as if themselves conveyanced via riverboat; as if
it wasn't me myself moving along, as if that wasn't
my decision. What I'd guess is plum blossom
trembles whitely against the icy
plum-and-slate of the abyssal night sky
as if in tacit refutation of a claim…
my claim, this squalid and
torturous charade, somewhere between
a cheapjack zoo and a Potemkin village built by Potemkin
to fool Potemkin, all the intricate tracery of imitation
only on the insides of the houses. From the outside
it looks an ugly concrete shambles, and anyway
for a Meiji bit this is skewing badly Bolshevik,
is it not, Pierre, rotating archly. I am
disgusted with myself.

I am disgusted with myself.

8KM

I.

The way the high noon sun strikes sparks from his spurs
as he skirts the corral, like a golden semaphore
from no one to no one. The horses
seem to sense his approach

and shift their weight from foot to foot, as if
in search of solid ground. Children scatter and reform. Prospectors
ask after one another's luck with a catch in the voice

as if the desert frit had got to the back
of their throats. Fear and anticipation mix like mongrel dogs in the street.
I've been holed up in my quarters,
practicing drawing my gun.

II.

The browned sawdust gathered in drifts against the the walls,
the Tamarack bartop – saturated and resaturated in spilled whiskey – smells
with the infinitely stale hungover smell of spilled whiskey.
The talk in the saloon's the same every night;

that's why I come here. The wash of the same words,
the recycled tropes, the lazy joust of boast and abuse,
it cleans me of the world, what's coming. But one time.
That poker game each man confessed he hates the taste

of chewing tobacco, as we sat, chewing our tobacco. Jardine
dead now, and McAndrew. Six grizzled pioneers, laughing like schoolgirls.
The candlelit ante of silver doubloons on the table
glittered like a shattering moon. Not to say a moon seen through tears.

CHF53/341x: Io shuttleport. Dregs of the system. Smell unreal: a citric, medicinal chisel which bypasses the sinus and lodges in the cerebellum. It's from their snackbar kiosks which, because the locals digest portions of their own flesh, vend seasonings and bandages. Dressings, is the joke. Sooner I can leave the better. CHFx channel partially degraded, signal dipping into noise.

CHF60/380x: At meeting point, beneath holomural depicting attack ship burning off the shoulder of Orion. The curl of the X-light stanchion off the shuttlestrip flames in Io's second sunset. Pretty, to a human. Such distraction precisely why I wouldn't be point-agent on this handover if I hadn't lied about profession. Would never taken job if not eviction. But focus. First reports of a new lifeform, even via text. Epoch defining. Purpose.

ChF37/223c: Contact established. Her disguise pitiful. Mine too. If we weren't so remote from the CoP we'd be discovered, all lost. Maybe all lost anyway. The port is a chaos. Uncontrolled multispecie young stagger and concoct, playbelieving, absurd as religion. Ignore.

KXN16/98p: Handover complete. Text legible by PTN2. Haven't had time to process, but…

CHF0/0a:

QQP04/31d: It's real. It is hard to believe. It's beautiful.

QQP120/882r: Difficult to paraphrase. Their demotic mutilated by antirealism, refusal of undeniable truths; conceptual translation bigger challenge than linguistic. Requires interpolation from impressionistic affective expressivity. Data encoded as mood. Appears these beings speak as if non-linear chronology, time all-present (immanent of the causal intra-action of matter?). Experience whole lives as one instantaneous and colossal detonation of feeling. Surely only a manner of speaking. Either way not *whole lives*. Cannot have discrete 'lives': texts imply cognition distributed across entire corporeal form – perhaps cf genus old-Earth cephalopod – but these at the level of cell, not brain, organ. Dividuals. And even this form ambiguously bounded. Implies diffuse mentation, denser or sparser clouds of qualia, overlapping across physically discrete beings. Wash of consciousness. Fractal identification, selves within selves within selves. A body could feel its *self* coming apart, every inch of torn-away surface a new site for the protozoa of aloneness to multiply, dance.

QQP42/294h: Can't conceive difference in chronological perspective. Non-linear time and free will logically inconsistent. No hindsight, no foresight. Is this an attempt to deceive?, withhold reality of situation? No discontent, no striving, no growth or change, loss. No moment of devastation. Hard to take seriously. A kind of strange beauty.

TZt22/160o: Total connection. Regret inconceivable. Pure intercourse between beings. Severance inconclusive. Contact departed. I do not think our songs will please them. Laughable mysticism.

ChF11/43x: But what if it is us who are wrong. My God.

8 KM

Like all the Achaemenid house Cambyses
had the features of a Persian but the eyes
of a Greek, as if reddened by a debauchery
of the creatures who breathe in the soul. Yes, you're right –

looking the supreme monarch in the face
is punishable by death, but in practice
us eunuchs of the harem escape the notice of his caste.
Until we present to them the balance of their books…

but you do not stand me these tankards of mead
to hear the intricacies of the court.
I travelled with Cambyses to fifty cities, eighty,
the gate-statues' hands worn to pencils by the infinite chain

of arrivals. And departures. Ah, Cambyses,
Sea-lord, King of Babylon. All-powerful and heirless.
The centre of a web of trade and levy
extending from Cathay to Athens, and childless.

Desperate, stalled in Agbatana, howling and gangrenous,
casting palmfuls of rubies about his chamber,
chewing his lips and his tongue into rags, knowing
he was dying and couldn't be. It falls

to me to re15/03/2020 i wish so much i could hold on to the
beauty of the walk back from furniss vale along the canal with
S, talking about the possible end of our relationship and the
sadness of the world and our love for one another. I can still
feel it now, reality in blue and silver, very real. i feel like right
now i am experiencing real life and nothing before or after

this moment will ever come close, any move i make will be a
withdrawal, and i only want to remain with the blue and silver
reallness and I remember
the Egyptian campaign,
the endless deserts, the sand

rising from itself like a god breathing,
or a demon. The horizon gauzy and trembling.
I trembled too. Endless days,
days of travel pestled to a paste of mesmer

by the heat, the sirocco's constant murmur, the boredom.
The days of battle I spent just as absent,
but out my stupor a sudden victory arose –
Egypt fallen and Cambyses pharaoh, Ra.

Or Osiris, blood-maddened, hacking to pieces
the sacrificial bullock and then, grim augur, the phalanx of
attendant priests, also. Perhaps
it wasn't gangrene. Some say he was poisoned.

Darius was his spearman, as well you know,
I think. Myself, I couldn't say.

The bar was decorated like the bar at the Dorchester. Chandeliers dripping ice like an overcompensating debutante. But they had the PA playing a Mountain Goats best-of. 'Cubs in Five', 'Up the Wolves', 'No Children'. Somehow it worked. The bar was empty, though. I looked down at my notebook, a single sentence on an otherwise blank page. I was trying to write about a child psychologist my father had met at a conference in Lima. She was famous in Peru for having written a study of a child. He had jumped out on a passerby with a toy gun and pretended to shoot, only for the man to fall down at just that moment and die. Thoracoabdominal aneurysm. But it wasn't going well. I felt trapped between the music and the notebook. Like a seam of coal compressed between two huge shelves of stone. The seam of coal had a headache.

Outside the afternoon was bright enough to have burned off the glamour from day-drinking. When I went outside for a cigarette. I thought about how 'cigarette' means a cigarette, and 'cigar' means a cigar, but 'cig' means a cigarette again. The central thing was being outflanked. I thought about how chess was just a game but supported real careers and lives for numerous people. I sipped my gin and tonic and squinted through my cigarette smoke into the declining but still sharp October sun. Due to some archaic holdover of Peruvian law a trial was conducted to determine whether the child *would* have been guilty, if he were an adult. Although the results of the trial would have no repercussions in the real world. It was just what might have been. And the kid was prevented by his legal guardians from ever finding out the result.

SECTION III: PEOPLE, COUNTRYSIDES

FOR SUCH A WIDELY USED MATERIAL, GLASS SURE DOES HAVE SOME DOWNSIDES

In the beginning it was cream and fucking
peaches.
          In the middle it was like finding a simile
so exact as to cease its working. Like finding an apple
with another, smaller apple in the middle.
In the early-middle it was like a bull in the
chinashop of my lazy preconceptions,
like a bull in the chinashop of my
clever reservations, like an
amateur kintsugi enthusiast in the ruined chinashop
of my childhood idealism. In the middle it was
peaches and cream, again, for a while. In the
middle it was like a glass filled with
glass beads. Like finding a heart with another
smaller heart in the middle. In the late middle,
intermittent stress and beauty in the
tigerstripe pattern of birch-forest in dense fog.
In the middle it was like mistaking
your reflection in a glass door for a person
reaching for the other handle, and standing
aside. In the middle, a delicate quadratics
of desire and satiety, the squaring of my need
by yours. In the middle the frantic chiming
of internal rhymes, like a dark shine of starlings
rising urgently together from the branches
of a pine tree. In the middle like opening a person
and finding another, smaller person inside. In the

OH 02:51AM,

I.

rough draft of 02:52, thatch
of biro ink and so close,
only an instant's lapse
of attention from true, but so soon
grown dank and leaden on that
low-grade grey recycled 80gsm
of the moment just past. Let alone

II.

the primordial ooze of
ten minutes back,
its still-viscous but ever-changing
terrain, roamed already
by the monstrous, alien forms
of you and I, then, agreeing
on what we thought was best.

YOUR MIND

the intricate architectural bric-a-brac of a second-world coastal town
a thousand years of colonisation and exchange
spilled like the contents of an overturned toy-chest
down the gentle hillside
from the ruined castle at its head
to the shore

the packs of feral cats at all the town's peripheries
flicker from vicious to adorable
and back

the pandemonium of market tat arrayed above the
medieval cobbles, the cartoon Rastafari
with *Cefalù* on their hats and burning joints
and the pornographic postcards
and all the wash of stuff I find degrading but which marks this as a space
to which by any fair definition I belong

love is very complicated

the desire to make you happy and the acknowledgement
that there are parts of your sadness I will never touch
and the inviolable barrier this either creates
or makes visible
and which love sweeps around
the way a stream ignores the rocks
which nonetheless dictate its
endlessly moving shape

PERHAPS

There were several interconnected points or nodes
webbed out like the hubs of a national railway
or a fat bushel of flickering christmas lights
lifted in two hands from their shoebox like a baby
from a blinking incubator and perhaps that was the moment

or one of the interconnected moments or nodes
or the golden beacons of pints across the snug
like a star sign or the nervous interstices of a body
probed by the Polish acupuncturist we punted on
in desperation and perhaps that was the place

or one of the interconnected places or nodes
which glow in like late-night cornershop off licences
to a drowsy cab fare or the over-jaunty upbeat
of every other bar as we listened mutely from our
side table at the wedding and maybe it was then

or one of several interconnected instances or nodes
like the tonal modulations in Mahler's Seventh's
changing keys each with a heart which reaches
tendrilous harmonic fingers into its neighbours' pockets
or the catch of the bitting on your father's heavy mortice
to roll the deadbolt home and perhaps that was it

or one of several interconnected occurrences or nodes,
supplementing or supplanting or corrupting one another,
or perhaps it never was lost. Although so many people are.

HEAD DOWN. KEEP FIT. AIM LOW.

A big pleasure is only its bigness, yak-stubborn
and full of itself, so packed with the butter of its own
cream there's no room for the cables, the modem, that little
letter-writing table to keep you in touch with the

sadness next door, the shame you were at school with,
the hope that moved to Melbourne in '04.
A jigsaw piece bigger than the jigsaw, unseeoutable from,
ungraspably slippery with the juices of its own excitement.

A small pleasure is a grass seed in a handful of grass seeds
flung amongst the rubble and rusted machinery
of your stalled and petty life, and finding the dark spaces,

the beads of lawless thought, to hoist their tiny flags
of anonymous moss green, content to be lost in the mass,
a gossamer of vanishing contentments, the lawn of an okay life.

130A WIGHTMAN RD

Like a shit angel sent dimensionally sideways
to sermonise on wildness or wilderness and closeness
that grey hole of a lockdown summer, a stray tom

took to visiting our back patio most days: he'd stalk up
whenever I was sat out reading or smoking
on the decking among upturned Hellmann's jar-lid ashtrays,
gins and tonic and rusted secateurs

and roll on his back as if he'd learned from the
pornstar cats on Instagram, and we'd feed him the expensive
cat biscuits from the plastic packages you bought
especially and then he'd slump onto his side

and purr scrappily through twenty or forty seconds
of contact behind his ears bitten as ragged as birch leaves
until some obscure tripwire got tripped
and he'd turn like a hellion, come up at you hissing, spitting,
tossing pawfuls of meathooky keratin,

and if the sermon was for everyone on earth
I don't know why it was he came to me, bewildered
among the Gs&T and bits of wire and the gleaming secateurs.

WE'RE NOT GIVEN TOO MUCH TO LOVE

The dream of language
curling like smoke in the
long skull of the last wild roan.
Semantics, semantics. The romance
of the imagined ascetic
wandering in the byways,
foolish and inconsistent. Semantics,
semantics. The note of vinegar
on your fingertips hours after
the chips on Margate beach – semantics. The
trepidation latent in the unflamboyant semaphore
of the over–fast tracked linesman:
semantics. *A priori* global murmuration:
semantics. Chess: semantics.
Tenderness: semantics! Hearty
signatories all. Oh semantics.
Oh the dark smiles of
menstrual blood under my fingernails
waking to an empty bed,
the semantics of a lover's leaving note

YES I KNOW WHAT IT'S SUPPOSED TO BE FOR, NO I'M NOT GOING TO STOP

Certainty is not a feeling but the description for a class of feeling.
Also not feelings: righteousness, sickness. And love, which is a propensity.
Everything visible is reflection, reflected light originating
elsewhere, certain wavelengths withheld like an unbroachable subject.
Nobody believes that belief matters more than action: nobody.
Or anyway they don't act as if they did.

Checkmate.

Why does the pre-emptive admission of my failures
in novel formulations and with metaphor from the structure
of experience not get me out of the wrongdoing which
follows inevitably

        like an afterglare. It's agony it's not enough.
If I say it hard enough that I am then it follows that I cannot be. Presto

chango. It is a pity that the very thing you are attempting to avoid
is encoded into the form of the argument you construct against it,
as if the barbarians could be simultaneously the cement between the
sandstone blocks of the great city walls.

Or almost as if. I do. I do.

Are two people in a relationship the way two people can be in a boat?
Or is the relationship just the people, changed a little?

Between parallel mirrors
the sacred point at which the reflections escape to infinity will always be
   hidden
by your own face. Hereby I name this ship

I will take out the bins, and I will try not to leave the keys
in the door, and I will continue
                                          to love you
to the fullest extent to which I find myself able. Oh love.
    Checkmate.

POEM IN WHICH IS IS SUFFICIENT

Sufficient unto the jenny
is the spin thereof. Sufficient unto the glaze
is the primer thereunder. Sufficient
unto the applecart is the upset
thereof. Sufficient unto the milk
the spillage, to the feeling its inspontaneous
overflow, and to the meltwater
the snow therefrom. Sufficient unto the forlorn hope
the momentary abeyance thereof. Necessary
but not sufficient to the roses
is the glass thereover; insufficient to the bread
are the roses thereby. Then again, the thin
delightful scraping of interpretation
to make palatable the things and ways
we come to, the churned butter
of concordance. Sufficient unto the wheat, too,
the chaff thereof, sufficient
unto the grist its revolving mill.
Sufficient unto the susan the
laziness thereof. Passing
muster the sufficiency the
fleeting recognition thereof. Sufficient unto a life
is the rub therein. Sufficient the startling lack
of a workable model
of sufficiency, and the specious
gesture laid thereover, Horatio. Sufficient
unto the apocalypse is the
endless forecasting thereof, the ensuing bacchanalia
and lassitude. Spill the applecarts! Reevaluate
Susan! Consume the meltwater icecream
in its marble chalice! For sufficient

unto the way is the passing thereby,
sufficient unto the will
must be the objects thereof. Enough
though, please: sufficient unto the words
is the speaking wherethrough
I meet your eyes, Sarah. Sufficient
unto the tall trees the tall trees'
receiving leaves, and the days, and the passing, and the
leaving and the passing and the light thereof.

THE FINEST FIRE-PROOFING WE HAVE

It's a poem about a young man insulating his family home,
written some time in 1929. It notices, the poem,
the knotted rope of his spine through his
flannel workshirt as he hunches to the skirting;
his intent fingers working loose the dark wood,
panel by panel, and pressing in material from the roll of

asbestos matting behind him. With love he does the work
that lovers do. With aching thumbs he rocks the tacks
back into their beds, as the poem tucks its nouns into their gullies,
investing itself as entirely as it can in how this fellow,
out of the dust of 1919, surrounds with love his
young fiancée, their love for one another. It drags and it dwells on this love,

it stalls and weeps for it, almost, this love inhabiting 1924
and written of in 1929. There's love in the way panels are pried up
and replaced. There's love in the way the panels are
pried up and replaced. There's love in the way the panels
are pried up and replaced. There's love [no,
one cannot now go back] in the way the panels are pried up and replaced.

There's love in the way the panels are pried up and replaced.

CROYDON PIVOT

Foggy morning: all the spidersweb in the world
steps forward, swagged with dew, bejeweled and sagging,
symmetrical and intricate and obsolete. They
strew the front gardens' either/or checkerboard:
mannered roses or a detritus of motorbike parts.
Like that's the choice: get ready to leave
or stay and tamper the genetics of the flora till it suits.

But diaspora's phenotype: the more made thing's
more natural. Can I stay with what I've made?
Writing a poem's like wrestling the commissar
for access to the castle's interrogation suite
and blasting yourself in the face with the lamp:
I have ways of making me talk. I am walked out
into the centre of a spiderweb: part spider, part fly.

On a paved road, no need
to attend to where
we place our feet; so it is
with the habits of thought

or romance. Is silence
replaced by sound, or does it
persist, the ghost of a ghost,
smiling, extending its hand?

SECTION IV: COUNTRYSIDES, PEOPLE

TWO WALKS (EROSION)

I.

A bad hunch, a worse correction, another hunch.
The country paths you fetch up on are not so much
paths as really more a diagram in sod-worn-to-clay
of the circular call of rural task or rather

really the desire lines of a will more material
than human or rather the unsettled spindles of water
run over the lost scutes of broken shale which are really
more the irresistible worrying of something
insoluble and sharp low in your attentive field

which is only really the play of colour over the surface of that
glassy incommunicado peach pit of self,
the meltwater rill and rivulet sculpted by a habit of slate

II.

Like humans, who are built
consolable, and then worked on,
this ten-yard spine of stone
exposed in its lonely sheep-field,

called to the permeable by incessant weather, is
inextricable from the weather,
the subatomic mizzle in rigidity,

slate-hue. This is the durable Wales of the soul,
for what that's worth, the whorling
of mica in basalt, the old demoglyphic psalm
of the mindless, the mineral, the undumb all

makes holding open a space in yourself for any caring to happen in so
so painful? For the articles of peace
and rational self-interest? Because it allows access to a form of happiness
inaccessible to the amoral? Because the
mental carapace required to weather the hardness
of indifference insulates you from what it means to be alive? Because
to generalise from your love for your friends makes the alternative
unthinkable? For special a priori reasons?
Because the conscience just magically won't
allow otherwise? To pre-emptively alleviate potential deathbed regret?
To get and remain on the right side of history?
Because it's possible to understand the sweetness
of pleasure as a kind of pleading? Because
your social group is such that articulable goodness
is a potent social capital?, and on a murky
semi-conscious level you believe that being good will somehow generate
endless mutually enriching oral sex? Because retaining the will to act and
    effect is really
the same as life in any meaningful sense?, the eyes of the unadopted dog
turning like a knife in the spirit? A knife in the spirit
is called an icicle. Because of birthday clothes? Because sorrow is always
    distributed
somewhat unevenly but never
entirely unevenly?, like a coal? Because inequality breeds
mental ill-health even in those
benefitting from inequality?, the humming Amstrad of the unconscious
unable to properly compute asymmetry? Because the avoidance of pain
cannot be made an end in itself? Just because of the underlying goddamn
structure of things? Does goodness have the keys to
a secret garden, sequestered from the palaver of concession?

Or does the underlying structure of that question
imply that goodness itself is concession? To uncouple
in the solvent of an irreligious morality the notions of
pleasure and guilt? To make up for plagiarising Joni? Because it's possible
    to understand
the sweetness of pleasure
as a kind of pleading? Because the backbone
makes a fine xylophone on which to
strum the planetary harmonies of ethics? For secret reasons? As
an example to others? What others? For the beauty
of the solidarity in the socialist songbook? For the
scouring rhetorical powerstance of anarchism? Because
the struggle is beautiful? Because the struggle itself is beautiful?

UNTITLED

The forest outdates its name by millennia
the river precedes its container the valley
and shame precedes its ostensible occasion
to obstruct any clear line of sight
between the trees in any given woodland
moss packed like clay around roots
disappearing into a mycorrhizal chatter
we're only beginning to understand
shame at earlier self   joy in markets of growth...
but no   the feathered things fleetingly
visible in the branches
the thick but near-inaudible whine of insect life
external counterpoint to the dense
sponge of nonhuman life exactly coextensive
with the humanity of the body   built of
void and monocellular beings
some muscle and neurones   maybe a sex organ
shame is the horror that we might be made up of what we're not
which we know really we aren't: shame
is the intimation of the horror upon repression's
unlatching   only
imagine if we could accept it   the final
end of humiliation   the interior walking in
fungal-matted clearings   globed in scented light
the plasticity of being   the cottage-industry of cognition
churning out steaming turnovers of shame and beauty
there's a paddling pool at the heart of this
ancient unexplored woodland believe me
it's not sophisticated but it's refreshing
it's hot and the day is long   don't be ashamed
of your gnarled feet   your cracked toenails
who else could do this   be exactly this   you, not you, either way

THEY DON'T MAKE A MIRROR FOR THE HEART

I.

Fuck always follow your heart, fuck
it wants what it wants, *fuck* that. The heart's
just as ego-gripped as all of you,
just as uttered by its own blood-and-guts mono-

mania, just as scored and raced, just as
blindsided by the hearts of others. It's just as
squat and myopic as all today's motorcade of
survivalist hysterica and vanity ploughed

through Goodwill city-centre. Oh trust the heart has its
slippery ways, the strange shifting in the viscera, gory
machination in the body politic, spies in the halls of all its lords.

II.

The roll of hillsides in pear and mint, crushed velvet—
soft   and seething with the inorganic formulae of excise,
humankind's millenarian agriculture of want.

YORKSHIRE HIKE

Dawn start, sleep and the fog of day's nativity
burning off as we ascend
into the good stuff of the cold Yorkshire
air, a breathing like being clean between
clean sheets. The good, rooty
meaningless greybrown of
off-season heather, the near
constant minor scree of off-soft sandstone
underfoot, the lacework of birdsong
perfuming the air. The drystone walltops'
moss flock a near-hallucinatory neon
chartreuse like a violin-line over the low purple
driven deep into the peaks' deep greens,
a Yorkshire chiaroscuro hard to notice
because it's what you look *from*, the same way
the magic-eye fields of lime and peat are always
already solved and awaiting dissolution – ah,
my world, the home green, the good ache
in the leg, the purer aspect of the
mild blade of spring chill, the sad laughter of sheep, roads
undulate with fidelity to landscape, the peaks'
bric-a-brac idiolect of fen violet and gritstone, humanity
settling in the valleys below us,
rich sediment, silt of the current of time
panned gently by time
for the gold of the moment, our being
where we belong. Dunfire. Slate. The ale of birdsong.

Dawn start, sleep and the fog of day's nativity burning off as we ascend
into the good stuff of the cold Yorkshire air, the gradated sky above the
horizon   like cloth, or lying

clean between
The good, rooty,
greybrown of
heather, the near
scree of soft
underfoot, a
birdsong perfuming
drystone-walltops'
almost
neon chartreuse
over the low
deep into the
greens a
chiaroscuro hard to
it's what you're
the same way
fields of lime and
already solved
dissolution. Ah,
world, the home
good ache in
the purer aspect
spring chill
of sheep, roads
fidelity to landscape
in the valleys below

the intestinal rhetoric
of belonging its pedant's
roll-call wilting the flora
to a jargon its own-brand
introvert imperialist scoring
borders onto the mappish
projections which waver
in the semiconscious
fostered on the colostrum
of brute repetition scrim-
shawing its shibboleth into
the bone ploughing your
self-worth into the soil
the manure of conviction
the community corkboard
stuck with the dizzying
local miscellania of
a personality no us without
a them the sine qua
non of stable being the
frothing fascist ideologue
crouched among the
faculties laying the roman
roads of habit & mannerism
the shut pub of the soul

clean sheets.
meaningless
off-season
constant minor
sandstone
lacework of
the air. The
moss flock an
hallucinatory
like violin-lines
purple driven
peaks' deep
Yorkshire
notice because
looking *from*,
the magic-eye
peat is always
and awaiting
this is our
green, the
the leg,
of the bladed
the sad laughter
undulate with
humanity settling
us, rich sediment,

silt of the current of time panned by time for the gold of moment,
our being where we belong. Dunfire. Slate. The ale of birdsong.

the intestinal rhetoric of belonging its pedant's roll-call wilting the

flora to a
own-brand
imperialist
borders onto the
projections
in the semi-
on the colostrum
repetition
its shibboleth
ploughing your
the
of conviction
corkboard stuck
local miscellania
no us without
qua non
the frothing
crouched among

the yorkshire propensity
to mock what you love
a showdown with inheritance
we are all one soul   trying
the counterlyric   con-
finement to a prelinguistic
solitude the spleen of even
temporary substance withdrawal
generally being caught up half
way the stuck-betweenness
jambalaya of insecure-avoidant
pride and the inside-out
knuckledusters hotpot rather
toad of self in the hole of self
intellectual insecurity arms race against
the unborn ghosts of critics but also
love, love, the fearful ca'canny, the shut pub
the ale of *birdsong*

jargon its
introvert
scoring
mappish
which waver
conscious fostered
of brute
scrim-shawing
into the bone
self-worth into
soil the manure
the community
with the dizzying
of a personality
a them the sine
of stable being
fascist ideologue
and

TRADE WIND

the twisting harmattan by which
eight words of an
alien script are swept
into the space in which your source-code
ticks through its
intricate subroutines – the gale of
preconception within which you
tremble and hunch, then
turn to bear its
ingenious mechanism of delivery
and flinch, and recover, –
it washes across your skin
like a cell-count, like the rake of
being named, of existing within
the misprisioning guess
of the passerby, that trade wind of
exchange that makes up
our mistakes, our emblematic internal
mannequin range – exchange
and appropriation, the
bijou space on which we've
pastured the sacred cow of our
dashing wrongness. What wine of belief
that we'll clear this up,
to be left blank
like an obelisk
and our handfuls of valuable gravel
and the rusk of self – that hamartial snake-eyed play to
expropriate the very levers
from out the papery cockpit
and fluke the launch codes
to blow the hell out of all this inbetween.

FORTY-NINE MOMENTS FOR THE SUBSTRATE

Moment, n. (3) A turning effect produced by a force acting at
a distance on an object.

Substrate, n. (2) The surface or material on or from which an
organism lives, grows, or obtains its nourishment.

'...I *felt* the great strength of *the page:* its ability, as a fibrous
surface, to *deflect* the *point* of my *pen.* The paper, and then *the
screen*, as weirdly *reflective*, repelling the ink or the *touch*.'
– Bhanu Kapil

Forty-nine sweet lapses
                            as the substrate
rears up through its foreground
to paw aside the small-talk of convention

and the brute matter of things
insists upon itself. The deft canvas
all the world is impastoed onto

booms and warps in the wallspace
behind the engine room of the faculties.
Forty-nine astringent objections
to the fair & lovely model

of necessity and established order. Forty-
-nine strange hurrahs for the substrate
and the bright matter of things

beats the rhythm of insistence
on the drum of its skin.
Forty-nine gaps in the gap of thought

things live in, from which the vehicle
bodies forth, scattering its tenor like

cloud, the rich feeling
uncoupling from the error
which begat it. Here. The bright patter of

thought against the rectangle
of skylight above you this autumn morning,
and the brute matter of the bright

pattern of surface and material
standing amicably by, and the substrate
laps sweetly

at the shore of all this
hall of the material's emanate moment.

SCENT OF AN ENDING

Imagine the ghostly, fluted architecture
of the physics we might've had
if only, furloughed to this Woolsthorpe orchard, the sun
angling and patterned on the dusty bark-lichen,
the shottish ache of lunch's overheavy suet,
Newton had noted the cone of scent left by his falling pippin.
It's an ontological chauvinism
for solidity over gaseous ways that persuades we live on
and not within
our planet. But we are: suspended
within Earth and breathing it, shot-through with its stuff,
saturated, crying it from the eyes,
towelling it into the hair, the feeling
as it accumulates at the backs of the knees,
swilling in the mitochondria, the quick blanks of idea,
in the insensible magnetism of the organs,
the sting of seawater on the soft palate
and the sting of the palate on the soft seawater,
the local strains of ultraviolet pattering on the dermis,
the autochthonic nature of thought and all things,
the slow hymn of energy lapsing into matter,
the suprageological swoon of entropy, the glacial
swoon of entropy, the dust
and sawdust aroma of a carpentry. The hill I suppose
I will die on
is that the smell of an apple is part of that apple. Or the hill we will all die on.

THE RUG JUST FROM PEOPLE WALKING ON IT

in collaboration with notes app on phone left unlocked in bag

The rug just from people walking on it
always ends up hiked against the skirting,
having shifted always in the same direction,
D intelligent e
Something to do with the weave or grain
of the c. VMexico cfc VBars. CX zxet,cc presumably. But
zone nzcçiiicxfxcxvx SDS x havec
such a bexxI zzxxeautiful tree outside your bathroo xz za x
xdcm window,
it's gt each cxx DX wanch. tching the thin svuxh cdCD
xfnlight, CDs dcfMv
little shovels of sunlightcx hvv v
to look at ç tb m the toilet Sz as xxxs x. UVXXX
a cherry tree, CVC cherries didn't get
very red in that specxwwa dsunlightgutuyc cucc fyexdzxsdgwwxs
nzsius
ific S fggg reewc
    1. d rf fb Fcvb vCCg of cherries ju .duE included
very bright, like unaccountably wonderful days
in a week ofog as drinkinwans nnsssnsnnh ug too heavily
and waking up on your xixwerexxxx again.. iii
B
HJ DX
The airplanes tracing their pretty
portents an vjd annihilation across categorically blue
skies, flowers dying explosively into the summer air

WHERE WE'VE GOT TO

Granted the words   a walk in the woods   are not like
walking in the woods but then

consider the parade of your past
faux pas and the ugly smart of unintended hurt,

the whole cavalcade of social misdemeanour whose
gross hiccupy return

doubles you over on the pavement:
how to empathise with those idiotic stricken models

of yourself?, dry-stone walls marking their
conceptual seams down the fall of hillsides like

the monuments of a gone people
whose routes toward beauty

still gossip from that wild site
below the diaphragm   and after all the memory

of   a walk in the woods   is not like
walking in the woods,

its dunfire colourway and clearings of 3G connectivity
and sweet messages from the new friends

it's still possible occasionally to make
and even keep – Beth, Dom, Nancy –

the fool of you evaporated, spiderswebs hung like
junk-shop jewellery in their dew, and

a walk in the woods is   nothing like
walking in the woods its small pauses,

the fallings into and from step:
presence, when you get
                                  right down to it,

crumbling at the slightest touch of attention to its
gearbox of constituent parts,

the gradated fields beyond the edges of the forest,
the damp-touched country signposts,

the tracks multiplying behind you in the path

CONCLUSION

Strip off the rough of treebark
for the clear sap of axiom;
electrify aluminium from the ore.

That it takes a village of humans
to raise an absolute, when within us each
is a five-foot post-berg Titanic of confusion
perpetually reformed so as to verge again
on breaking up,

like a glacier. The ideal ratio in architecture
is based on the proportion of the human form:
so it is with the lacework of decline
we levy on the subjects of our disquisition,
the grass dying in our footsteps. That we

build our ship-in-bottle model and,
done, fold
keening to the kitchen floor in
despair at the worldly absence of
corresponding original; rage, demand
restitution from the universe
in the brusque cash of certainty –

environment's greenscreen simply
coming apart under the combined human requirement

for an absolutism nothing real could sustain. From counting fingers
to decimation. An image
is only a slice of the world,
a freight-car with its couplings knocked off,

a treebranch stripped of twigs for a walking pole.

UNTITLED

On a paved road, no need
to attend to where
we place our feet; so it is
with the habits of thought

or romance. Is silence
replaced by sound, or does it
persist, the ghost of a ghost,
smiling, extending its hand?

SECTION V: [...]

FATHERLAND

(…and of course the blind is blind for deeper blind,
metaphor metaphor for more than we can take:

the words decay, Gilgamesh and Sylvia
kiss in the cupboard of every limerick.

When it comes to loss the scales go funny:
in the dark the similes switch polarities,

the rivermouth frays into delta, estuary,
a loosening braid of currents in the tide.

We dread the fatherland abstractly, but oh
its embassies, here in the country of the living…)

TWO MORE UNEDITED FIRST DRAFTS

I.   09 October 2021, Croydon

Thank Christ the last parts of anything don't matter;
it's always the rushed lacquer,
useful, okay, for sealing in what's already there,
but certainly it's adding nothing new.

The you that you're not drip-feeds its sticky data
into the paddling-pool of consciousness you splash in,
terminal and preternatural and agog. Yes! Cry all you like,
you're a ham grandstanding to a rake of sighing doppelgangers,

and inside the ham, more ham. You're a conman
stripping the huddled OAPs that are
your older selves of their
paltry building society accounts of soul,

a soul which has accumulated over decades like a moss.
You think you just get given that stuff? Bunkum.
Sometimes I think you spend it, handing out at the end of each thing
a little party bag of your precious essential self never to be returned.

Oh, never to return? Really? Grandstander. It's all cyclical,
a little wheel on a wheel of wheels, somewhere between
those nuts scriptural angels and a vast for-the-tourists mandala;
a contact point. Or perhaps not: walk down any

tree-lined path with your neck craned back; follow
the polygraph zig-zag of sky where the leaves of the trees
on opposite sides of the path refuse to touch. They just

will not touch. Is this the way of things? The clever statuary waits

numbly, imperious, each hoping for a lightning bolt to pitch it
into its neighbour? Bleak. I hope you enjoyed the first parts.

II.   30 January 2017, Sorrento

Thank Christ the first parts of anything
don't matter; it's always the rush matting
of words over the rich dirt, the word for a thing
ringing out before that thing arrives.

Don't panic, all of this can be redrafted later.
We can add imagery, charming phrases,
tell one another we're in love. Many species
remain unextinct. Some are even thriving.

WORLD AUBADE

'I must be gone and live, or stay and die...'

Romeo and Juliet, Act 3 Scene 5

Wilt thou be gone? What light, I guess, through yonder
window breaks: it is the east and capital's the sun,
the plastic knick-knacks scattering the dresser
teeming in its light with properties

Our hands are slick with the oil of peaches

peaches and

the world is growing brighter, some unseen finger
holds fast-forward: it grows
brighter yet, whiteout stark, and yet it is
not daylight, it is
some meteor the sun exhales; we must
decide, my world, whether we can part or how

or when, my everything and with
what attitude must I face thine father,
what aspect, dick still wet
with the waters of the nonhuman   oh God,

what does it mean to love something so full
of pain and the knotweed of dread,
arpeggiating like a broken thrush the registers of grief,
slick with the oils of chauvinism and charisma,
pilgrims washing up on the beaches. My love will
kill you, kill us. Kill us all.

this story we cannot do without, and cannot
retell. This evil eye we bought
and cannot now resell so it accretes like the polyvinyl-
chloride princesses on the sideboard. The horde
of the inhuman, the bestial all,
her vestal livery is but sick and green
and none but fools do wear it. The birds sing
but no longer mean it. The birds would sing
and think it were not right. What sweet sorrow
to persist within this disappeared world

ACKNOWLEDGEMENTS

Thanks to the editors of publications where these poems have previously appeared: *Poetry Review*, *PN Review* and *The Tangerine*. 'Head Down. Keep Fit. Aim Low.' was commissioned as part of DINA's small pleasures project. 'Forty-nine Moments for the Substrate' was commissioned by Arts Council England to accompany their exhibition 'On Paper'. The first draft of 'Perhaps' was originally written on the Rough Trade Books/Soho Radio programme *Stress Test*.

Thanks too to the people who've read and provided feedback on these poems: Martha Sprackland, Alex MacDonald, Jane Yeh, Dai George, Rali Chorbadzhiyska, Stephen Nashef, Beth Underdown, Matthew Hollis and, particularly, Chrissy Williams and Jemima Foxtrot. John McAuliffe is as good an editor as I can imagine, and I am thankful. Thanks to Sarah Vincent.

Thanks to the writers and others I've stolen from unattributed, including but not limited to William Shakespeare, Jennifer Aniston, Ta-Nehisi Coates, Lucretius, Gore Vidal, Kurt Vonnegut, Philip K. Dick and Tracy Emin.

Love and thanks to my family, and my friends Nancy, Nadia, Rosa, Tom and Madii.

Douglas Adams, *Life, the Universe and Everything* (Pan Macmillan)
Dante Alighieri, *Paradiso*, translated by Henry Wadsworth Longfellow
Nuar Alsadir, *Animal Joy* (Fitzcarraldo Editions)
Nuar Alsadir, *Fourth Person Singular* (Liverpool University Press)
Jennifer Aniston, interviewed by Leslie Bennetts,
    https://archive.vanityfair.com/article/2005/9/the-unsinkable-
    jennifer-aniston
Jane Austen, *Emma* (Penguin)
Francis Bacon, interviewed by D. Sylvester,
    https://theoria.art-zoo.com/interview-with-david-sylvester-
    francis-bacon/
J.G. Ballard, *Crash* (HarperCollins)
Anne Carson, *Float* (Cape)
Teju Cole, *Blind Spot* (Faber)
Zelda Fitzgerald, *Save Me the Waltz* (Vintage)
Michel Foucault, *The Order of Things*,
    translated by Alan Sheridan (Routledge)
Jean Genet, *Our Lady of the Flowers*,
    translated by Bernard Frechtman (Faber)
Amitav Ghosh, *The Great Derangement* (University of Chicago Press)
Louise Glück, *Averno* (Carcanet)
Johann Wolfgang von Goethe, *The Sorrows of Young Werther*,
    translated by David Constantine (Oxford University Press)
Stuart Hall, *Familiar Stranger* (Penguin)
Byung-Chul Han, *The Expulsion of the Other*,
    translated by Wieland Hoban (Polity Books)
Robert Hass, *Twentieth Century Pleasures* (ECCO Press)
Martin Heidegger, *Basic Writings*, edited by David Farrell Krell,
    translated by Frank A. Capuzzi and J. Glenn Gray (HarperCollins)
Sheila Heti, *Motherhood* (Harvill Secker)
Bhanu Kapil, *How to Wash a Heart* (Pavilion/Liverpool UP)

Clarice Lispector, *The Passion According to G. H.*,
    translated by Idra Novey (Penguin)
Lucretius, *On the Nature of the Universe*,
    translated by Ronald Melville (Penguin)
Andrew Marvell, 'The Garden'
Karl Marx and Friedrich Engels, *The Communist Manifesto*
    (translated by Samuel Moore)
George Meredith, 'Modern Love: L'
Kei Miller, *There is an Anger that Moves* (Carcanet)
Czesław Miłosz, *New and Collected Poems 1931–2001*,
    translated by Czesław Miłosz and Lawrence Davis (Penguin)
John Milton, *Paradise Lost*
George Monbiot, *Feral* (Penguin)
Michel de Montaigne, *The Essays*, translated by M. A. Screech (Penguin)
Alice Oswald, *Memorial* (Faber)
Helen Oyeyemi, *Peaces* (Faber)
Plato, *Timaeus and Critias*, translated by Desmond Lee (Penguin)
Marcel Proust, *Sodom and Gomorrah*,
    translated by Moncrieff and Kilmartin (Vintage)
Marcel Proust, *The Fugitive*, translated by Moncrieff and Kilmartin (Vintage)
Adrienne Rich, *Arts of the Possible* (W. W. Norton & Company)
Anil Seth, *Being You* (Faber)
Karen Solie, *The Caiplie Caves* (Picador)
William Thackeray, *Vanity Fair*
Tomas Tranströmer, *The Half-Finished Heaven*,
    translated by Robert Bly (Penguin)
Simone Weil, *Gravity and Grace*, translated by Arthur Wills (University
    of Nebraska Press)
Ludwid Wittgenstein, *Culture and Value*, translated by Peter Winch
    (The University of Chicago Press)